Chasing Dragons in Moravia

By

G. Michael Vasey

Table of Contents

The Shaman's Final Message

When I was writing the precursor to this little book which I called *'Chasing the Shaman[1]'*, I was excited by a significant change in my feelings about living in the Czech Republic. I felt that I had finally made some sort of a spiritual connection with the land after living here some 14 odd years and this then had a ripple effect throughout my life. I was also very aware of the number of coincidences or synchronicities building up in my life and I have always seen that as a sign of being in the flow and on the right path. I have often called this *'the magic.'* In the weeks following the publication of *Chasing the Shaman*, to maintain the momentum. I had begun to engage in an exercise that I had suddenly dreamed up based on something I had read in an Alan Richardson book called *'Dark Magery'*[2]. It was an extension of what I had already started, but with more deliberate intent and it was to have a further powerful impact.

---

[1] Chasing the Shaman. The Magic of Connecting with the Land. G. Michael Vasey, Asteroth's Books, 2020

[2] Dark Magery, Alan Richardson, Amazon, 2020

It was to engage with a set of Slavic deities in an imaginative way.

Meanwhile and strangely enough, almost immediately the *Chasing the Shaman* book was published, the actual shaman that I had 'chased' ceased his activities. Was that related? I do not know. Other than the first time, when I bumped into him in mid flow, I had never managed to catch him doing his thing. I wanted to. I had so many questions for him. However, one day as I walked through the area where he left his stone markings, I saw that he had moved all of his stones to areas both sides of the gravel seating area and arranged them in heaped patterns. For days on end, there was no change in these arrangements and no tell take sign of ash, cigar or roll ups left on or around the stones. I was a bit disappointed because as I said, I had really wanted to meet this shaman.

One day a bit later, I noticed that where the major stone design had usually been placed, all the stones had now gone. I checked the other side of the gravel area and found the arrangement was still there. I felt a tremendous sense of anguish realizing that whatever this chase had meant, it was now over. There seemed little doubt that this design located where it was, was simply the end game of whatever his purpose had been.

I held onto the metal fence and leaned over it to get a better look – nope, no tobacco either. Damn! It was then I noticed that on the top metal bar, between my hands, there were words painted on the bar. I had never seen them before! Could it be a message?

Unfortunately, the middle of the phrase was a bit smudged, but I photographed it anyway. I checked all along that fence in the area and found no more writing anywhere else. It didn't look like graffiti and the writing was aligned exactly with the site he had used and where the stones still lay. Further investigation led me to realize that the location where he had hammered a hole and placed a polished pebble in it right at the beginning of our chase (which I now realize was some sort of marker), was directly in line with the stone arrangement on the other side of this metal fence and also with the site where his stones had usually been arranged. Not only that, but his stone arrangements were always aligned in this direction too. So this writing seemed significant.

"S*lysim sum tve xxxx ve svem tele*," it said.

I knew what the individual words meant but what was the missing smudged word?

I showed it to one of my Czech friends who managed to decipher the missing word as '*krev*' – blood.

"I can hear the flow of your blood also in my body"

Was it a message? Was it for me? Was it just part of whatever ritual the shaman had been engaged in? Was it written there by some other person and if so, why? (and if it had, it was some weird message for a teen intent on graffiti) Lots of questions.

What did it mean? Interestingly, my Czech friend, who I have been taking along on some of my trips and encouraging a little bit, made a brilliant observation. He said can't you hear your blood flowing when meditating? Your heartbeat? And, if all is one, why couldn't he hear yours flowing too? This made sense to me. Connection.

Connection with the Shaman?

On the other hand, blood can be thought of as lifeblood or life itself.

I can hear the flow of your life even in my body.

Again, this could be a connection with the shaman and that he was aware of the flow of my life? It has always seemed a bit weird that I had a sense that the shaman knew I knew and that a game was being played out between us. I always felt as if he visited the stones just before or after me and that I was being observed. Perhaps he had a primary goal and dragging me along for the ride was secondary but none the less, I am convinced he knew. In fact, we had played a little game of energizing pebbles in the sun. He moved my pebble to where his was and I moved it back again.

As I reflect back, it seems to me that a lot of what I did in terms of research and found through my interactions with the landscape and its history and energy stemmed in part from the interaction with this unknown shaman. I do believe that this was deliberate on his part, but I cannot prove it. Whatever, the shaman was the catalyst for my own activities, and he did awaken in me a bit of a shaman I never knew I had and for that, I am grateful.

Finding Perun

I had been reading Alan Richardson's Dark Magery book and he gave me an idea. One that I thought fit quite well with what I was interested in and also in helping to build a connection to this foreign and Slavic land. By now, I was reading avidly about the Slavic Gods and also a lot of Slavic fairytales, myths and legends. If you overload on these things, they begin to invade your psyche anyway so what better than to do some rudimentary God form work? I had never really tried it before. Well, not in a consistent and deliberate fashion. So why not give it a try?

From what I can gather, Slavic mythology and the Slavic gods originate from Proto-Indo-European mythology and emerged in the 2nd to 1st millennium BCE. As may be expected then, they bear some resemblance to Norse, Celtic and other mythologies and pantheons.

The Slavic gods were probably most widely worshipped just before the adoption of Christianity in 988 BCE. However, I had already determined that the conversion to Christianity was mainly at the level of the aristocracy and that belief in the old gods continued among the commoners for many, many more years. This is seen at Hostyn[3] where baby Jesus is depicted as a baby Perun in what I believe to be a nod to the locals. Pagan stalwarts survived around the region for a long time.

Another thing to note is that there were three Slavic areas including the East Slavs (Russia), South Slavs (Bulgaria, Croatia and parts of Bosnia) and West Slavs (Czechia, Poland etc.). Some of the Slavic deities were known only to one or two parts of the Slavic region.

The Slavs also did not build or use churches or temples. Rather, their religion was a part of daily life and they felt the gods could be venerated anywhere. Mostly it seems this veneration and worship took place in nature and outdoors. Since little was written down and few sites preserved, a good deal of

---

[3] See Chasing the Shaman

guessing and conjecture has taken place along with forgeries like the Book of Veles, for example.

For a few days then I began knocking on Perun's door. Perun is the Slavic God of thunder and one of the most important in the pantheon and I will come back to him shortly in more detail. I must say, at first, I got nothing much at all and was rather disappointed but then one night, I had some very strange dreams and then in short session where I took on the form of Perun in my imagination, some very strange thoughts.

These 'thoughts' or insights arrived in my mind as a seed thought and then exploded into a number of strands. In a meditational state, it is possible to follow all of the strands all at once but on coming back to normal consciousness, these quickly fade unless written down.

What I sensed, or received, was that the Slavic culture of that time was really quite alien in terms of its concepts of life and death compared to now. I got the idea that death was not that much of an issue as for them the shadow side of life existed in balance and harmony with that of the living. Life and death were two sides of the same coin and the transition between them was subtler somehow. I could see how, for them, the ancestors were a real and shadowy presence in their daily lives. Suddenly, my shaman started to make sense. He was working this subtly and maybe, just maybe, showing me the way?

For the Slavs of that era, the veils were thinner and more subtle and the influence of the otherworld more obvious in their lives. Perhaps today we would think that life for them was held in scant regard and was cheap, but this I feel would be a tremendously wrong simplification. The feeling I got was that the afterlife or the underworld was there – a very thin veil separated the two – so it wasn't that life was cheap – it was in fact venerated – but when you sense that the afterlife is right there and almost visible or accessible – then the transition from living to dead simply isn't the massive thing we would think of now. Death was really just a transition from one state to another more shadowy but still as real a state of being as being alive. This strange sense of living alongside the dead and 'never lived' was truly an alien feeling that entered into my perception and I cut short the session to write about it before I lost that sense altogether. It seemed to me to be an 'aha' moment sitting there in meditation assuming the form of Perun in my mind.

Perun, of course, is counterbalanced by Veles, the Slavic God of the underworld and the two are perpetually fighting but essentially a balance is maintained via this conflict as gains and losses are made by both sides throughout the annual cycle. These two worlds exist side by side and the thinnest of veils separate them at either end of the mighty Oak tree that for Slavs, symbolized the world. Perun and Veles are a duality – a sort of ying and yang and actually that is common within the Slavic pantheon.

I am a man that never saw much value in developing a physique, but the other part of taking on the form of Perun is the bulk of muscle and now I rather regret not having buffed up a bit. It actually feels pretty good to be muscular even if only in the imaginative mediational state! However, it was the realization of how alien a world the Slavic world may have been by modern standards that most permeated my consciousness.

What this helped me to understand is how transient things are and how the current emerging culture of the politically correct, avoidance of any perceived offensiveness and so on, seems to be totally at odds with the ability to make spiritual progress; despite what some people may believe. It is actually only through being offended, hurt, wounded, and so on, that we learn and grow, so to avoid that cosmetically or to simply deny it, seems counterproductive. In particular, this recent habit of looking back in time and judging its characters by today's supposedly superior standards and condemning our ancestors as racists and so on, is also actually counterproductive – they lived in their time, to their standards and we have no basis with which to judge either them or the times they lived in. Rather, we should perhaps seek to understand their environment and learn from it?

I am increasingly convinced humanity is on the wrong journey as the trend in new ageism is towards some nirvana or utopia of meaninglessness that will eventually turn out to be a hell on Earth. Back in the times of the Slavs, spirit was near, the transition to death and life subtler. Little value was placed on material possession and I suspect shamanic magic was very real. They lived in nature – within the realm of the Goddess and between the combating Gods of the over and underworld. Life could be cruel, short and tough and they knew the Goddess in both of those aspects.

Before going further, I want to talk about this useful method of adopting a God form. It sounds like some sort of sophisticated ritual and for some, perhaps it is. For me though, it comprised learning as much as I could about the particular form to be adopted – physique, looks, habits, personality, associations and so on. Based on that, I could build a mental image of the God in my mind standing in front of me. I imagine the back of the God form first – its easier. Then the front – the facial features and so on. Once, I have imagined this image in as much detail as I can, I step in and become it (before attempting, please take all the usual precautions). The third or fourth time I do this, I don't spend much time imaging the form as somehow I already have it in mind. I simply become it. This means using the imagination – how does it feel to be a muscular God? How does it feel to wield an axe? And so on.

There is a point, at least for me, where this becomes an effortless transition. I am the form. I can do this walking through the forest or walking down my street. I am always amazed when suddenly, a stream of thoughts enter my head as a result of this imaginative transition. Always.

What about Perun? What did I learn about Him in my research?

According to Encyclopedia Britannica, Perun is the thunder God. He is a *"fructifier, a purifier, and the overseer of right and order. His actions are perceived by the senses and seen in the thunderbolt, heard in the rattle of stones, the bellow of the bull, or the bleat of the he-goat (thunder), and felt in the touch of an axe blade. The word for Thursday (Thor's day) in the Polabian language was 'peründan'. In Polish* 'piorun' *and in Slovak* 'parom' *denote "thunder" or "lightning.""*

He is also apparently the patron of soldiers and noble warriors. According to myth, even as a baby, he demonstrated his powers and a temper, and there are stories about him overcoming great trials and challenges. He was taken to the underworld as a child where he slept as his family searched for him. He became a man during his sleep in the underworld, rising up and after many challenges, found his way back to his home in the heavens. There he met the Moon Goddess and married her and became the head of the Slavic pantheon of deities.

Perun is associated with the oak tree, four leaved clover and the iris, among other plants. He is also associated with Thursday (Thor is like Perun in the Nordic pantheon), His numbers are 4 and 8 and his metal is Tin. Other associations are mountains, fire, (I would add air) eagles, doves, horses and carts, the hammer, axe and arrows, and war. There is also some equivalency with St. Michael as both are commanders of heavenly armies that fight and conquer the underworld deity. Perun is associated with thunder, lightning, storms, and rain, and represents strength, courage, protection, justice and fertility. He is the God of law and order, law enforcement, protection and even, democracy.

His sacred days are thought to be the 2nd of February and the 2nd of August. February 2nd is Candlemas, and it is tradition for Slavs to carry "thunder candles" to church. These are large candles that are blessed with protective powers and only burned on special occasions. However, as a result of the calendar shift that occurred in 1918 in Eastern Slavic lands, there is some disagreement, some see July 20th as Perun's day.

As I assumed Perun's form, I often had images of being in a heavy forest and yet under the sky along with a strong sense of being at home there and wanting to be out in nature. I also saw Eagles soaring or sometimes, Eagle's wings. I was often filled with energy. I gathered this natural fiery energy and released it again as lightning. Lightning is often called '*Perun's arrow*' and the places where it strikes are thought to be where evil spirits hide. Trees struck by lightning are treated with respect and the wood of such trees is used to make the magical implements by people in the Carpathian mountains.

I also learned that the best way to conduct my meditations and god form assumptions was in nature itself. I would go for a walk and as I walked imaginatively become one or the other of the two gods. Then, as I walked, the forest would take on an entire new sense of being. I can only use the word magic to describe this. Everything became more alive, more colorful, filled with energies and creatures would interact with me in ways I had never before experienced.

Once, I felt as if I was riding chariot and doing just what was needed to maintain order. There was no feeling of love in this at all. It was simply my duty to restore order out of chaos - whatever that took. No sentimentality at all. Again, I had this overwhelming feeling that justice in the eyes of the Slavs was not based on sentimentality or misplaced emotions – it was a bloody and swift justice. Very unlike the sentimentality of modern new ageism, which I now think of critically as an undesirable trend as a result of these activities. Order is maintained through strength by Perun not via sentimentality. He applies the law, and the law is blind to circumstance or happenstance. In that sense, there is an aspect of Geburah about him I feel. He is, after all, the god of order, justice and law.

In another session, I saw Perun as a mighty and crowned man. He was crowned with the Sun and as I saw this vision in my mind a butterfly danced around me and then landed on me - in reality. In fact, as we will see, butterflies were a feature of these meditations along with the doves, who were everywhere as well, almost dive bombing me as I walked in the form of the muscular warrior Perun. I also thought that this vision showed that there was a solar aspect to our Perun.

Another evening slowly walking around the Castle in Brno, I had to stop, sit and bask in the Sun as it lowered toward the horizon. I was bathed in heat and light, and I started to think again about Perun gathering energy slowly and then releasing it suddenly. He had done so the night before in a huge storm and I had photographed him in the skies spitting and snarling with anger. As my exercises with Perun continued, I began to notice that the weather had been remarkably thundery in the region (more so than previous years) and that I had been feeling a lot of, well, anger. Maybe this anger that I felt was a reflection of his anger? Maybe my anger had been slowly building while focusing on Perun and would also suddenly discharge somehow?

On many occasions, as I walked being Perun, a beautiful butterfly or several butterflies would appear from nowhere and dance around my head. Sometimes, it landed briefly on me and then disappeared only to reappear a little ways down the path. On some occasions I sat and watched the butterfly dance its fluttering dance several times almost landing on my head. I have never seen a butterfly behave this was before and so I took note. Apparently, the butterfly represents spiritual rebirth, transformation, creativity, endless potential, vibrant joy, change, ascension, and an ability to experience the wonder of life. Suddenly, butterflies became abundant in my life. They were everywhere, in every color and form, fluttering around me and this lasted through to early October – a time when I thought butterflies should be long gone.

For me, a Butterfly represents joy, happiness, transformation. I'm reasonably happy and I have transformed in recent months becoming happy with alone time and living alone, but I fear I'm also angry and not joyful. Perhaps the Butterfly is a signal to remind myself to be joyful and to let things be. Anger over what other people think, how they behave and believe doesn't do me any good and doesn't do anything at all to them. Why this angers me I haven't truly gotten to the bottom of. It's not a control issue. It's more a 'can't you see the truth when it is staring you in the face' sort of thing. It's not my problem really.

Maybe the Butterfly is saying that I should focus on my spiritual world and express the joy that I feel when in nature in my entire life? When in nature, I'm filled with a deep love and awe of what I see around me, and I am joyful because of it. It is only when I have to deal with other humans that I become angry and morose.

The answer isn't to become isolated. I think the answer is to care less about others – their thoughts, actions and interactions. Not to care less about them as people but to allow them to live. To be joyful for them.

Butterflies were not all I noticed. Doves suddenly seemed to notice me too as stated above. On one walk, I stopped for a while to look over the city and photograph for the 1000th time the Cathedral on the hill opposite bathed in sunlight. It was at this point that I noticed the grayish colored birds swooping and diving between the trees. At first I thought they were pigeons, but then realized I had never seen pigeons flying like this and so I looked up these birds – doves! Again, I wondered what a dove might represent? I later read that the dove brings forth a calming presence in times of pain, strife, and difficulties. It signifies love and peace, and it serves as a messenger or a liaison between your thoughts and your reality. It reassures you that love, and grace will always be in your life and there will always be that promise of something beautiful and meaningful. It's apparently a wake-up call for you to be in touch with your spirituality and to develop your higher self.

How apt I thought as I walked a little further and watched as a dove dive bombed me just to make sure I understood it was there for me in that moment.

In his work to maintain order, I also detected a voracious appetite for life. Eat, drink and be merry – yes and womanizing too. Perun sort of overlaps a bit with Thor in this respect. He is a very manly figure, and one senses he is full of testosterone. Yet there was balance and above all, order. Balance and order, and a sense of great joy in everything – in creation. Another insight I got was that while Perun was responsible for maintaining order in creation he was not its Creator. He was a sort of governor or maintainer.

Another entry in my diary comes from a dream I had during the period I was assuming Perun. It was a very vivid dream, and I awoke murmuring the words '*Sol Invictus.*' I immediately Googled this term knowing that it meant '*Unconquered Sun*' but very little more. It relates to Sun worship and appeared to me to confirm the solar aspect of Perun and, being associated with Jupiter as well, the King of the heavens and Lord of the Earth. Jupiter was also known in Greece as the God Zeus and as we know, Perun is the thundering God of the Slavs.

Perun came through to me very strongly as a solar God. He saw right and wrong in absolute terms – again there was no sentimentality in him at all. He was swift to anger and quick to strike. He was fire and air – often fire in the air! He was fiery. He showed me that in times gone by, the living and the dead coexisted and were aware of one another. Nature was a part of everyday life and the Goddess was respected – not just because she was beautiful but because she could also be terrible. He imbued a shamanic quality within me that I had never really felt before – a deep sense of peace and respect for the Goddess and nature – a yearning to be with the Goddess, to know her, to feel her presence in my life and to celebrate that. I often felt as if I would wander in the densest part of the forest where I would meet her and be swept to some other place never to return. Nature took on this bright and ethereal quality. I felt a sense of love and longing for it, for her, facilitated by Perun himself.

Perun, Thor, Zeus are all thunderer gods. They may share common roots or perhaps they originate in the human psyche springing to life muscular, raw and potent. They are there to maintain order and the law which they do with a gusto and raw masculine energy. They are fiery and have a temper. They can be angry and seek revenge. Yet, in the background, one gets a sense that this god serves the goddess. She's the boss behind the scenes.

Atilla and Earth Energy

Most weekends, I seek out nature and Earth energies. Even during the COVID lockdown, visits to nature were allowed in the Czech Republic and so I went to the forest as often as I was able or for a walk around the Castle above me. Even on occasions where I was in Hungary visiting my girlfriend, we would seek out nature and the mysteries. One Sunday, we went off in search of a place called Atilla's Hill or Dome. In Hungary, Atilla occupies a place of pride. Well, he would, wouldn't he, being a 'Hun' and all, scourge of the Romans?

The Atilla's Hill location is supposed to be the site of his wooden palace building but in reality, who knows. There are other claimants and being cynical, in attracting tourists and people interested in healing, the owner does well from this assertion. Despite my skepticism, something of significance was found in that location in archeological work though, and that was a handmade golden deer figurine that now resides in the Hungarian National Museum. This deer figurine dates back to the right period of time and therefore lends supports to the idea that Atilla may actually have occupied this area.

The mound is located outside of Budapest in the countryside at a place called Tápiószentmárton and we found it just a little difficult to find, but we succeeded after a couple of wrong turns. The actual site is part of a horse farm called Kincsem Lovaspark and before that it used to be a Russian airfield. However, even before that, it was famous for breeding horses. One huge claim to fame is that it is the birthplace of a famous horse called Kincsem. According to Wikipedia...

Hungarian for "My Precious" or "My Treasure";
March 17, 1874 – March 17, 1887) was
a Thoroughbred racehorse who has the most wins
of any unbeaten horse in the history of the sport,
having won 54 races from 54 starts. The next
closest such record belongs to Black Caviar, with
an unbeaten record of 25 wins from 25 starts.
Foaled in Kisbér, Hungary in 1874, Kincsem is a
national icon, and is highly regarded in other parts

of the world too. Over four seasons she won against both female and male company at various racetracks across Europe, including Classic race wins in the Austro-Hungarian Empire, and major stakes victories in Germany, France and England. As a broodmare, she has proved a lasting influence on the breed, with modern descendants including English Classic winners Polygamy and Camelot.

The man who purchased the land soon discovered something special about the place noting a certain 'energy' and seeing that the horses always laid in a certain area. Pretty soon, it developed a reputation for healing and I'm sure the owner saw an opportunity developing his horse farm, hotel, horse museum and Atilla's mound commercially as a place for healing. Some commentators have remarked that it may all just be a ploy to make money, others have pointed to a tie in with a resurgence of Hungarian nationalism (apparently the place is littered with nationalistic statements). What interested me was the reputation for healing energy and a couple of write ups mentioning [4] a ley line referred to as the George line, crossing the location as in this example.

"As a result research started. The scientists' measurements revealed a beneficial energy-radiation, which is facilitating healing processes in the human body. The centre of this energy-flow is on the Attila mound, but its curative effects can be felt on the entire territory of the Kincsem Equestrial Park.

The sacral lines as eg. the St. George-line or the Ley-line are also constituting part of the primeval-energy, found in the park. The scientists have not yet reached to an exact conclusion, whether these energies are already known or there is an underlying force behind the observed peculiarities and manifestations. It is well known that all illnesses result from a state of energy-deficiency. This radiation helps to recover the split balance in

---

[4] http://www.kincsemgolf.hu/eng_attilamound.htm

a way, that it does not affect only one organ but harmonizes the energy-flow in the whole body. Since then, quite a lot of people have recovered, they love this place and are grateful for getting back their health. A very poignant example of gratitude was when during one night in the spring of 2001 a stranger has placed a statue of the Virgin and a bunch of flowers on the mound. KOCSI János, the successful entrepreneur, proprietor of the park, who devoted the entire 2001 to research has said: "for these very moments, I simply cannot regret spending so much time, money and energy on research.""

I can find no other references at to a 'George line' nor to any 'scientists' writing about the place. I did confirm that the golden deer was found there. Even so, it seemed an ideal place to visit and explore. I would determine if I could feel any energy and go from there.

As we arrived, a huge thunderstorm started. We paid and went in in the car and parked by the mound. The car park had many empty vehicles in it and another car was full of people also waiting for the storm to pass. We waited and waited. After 45-minutes and a check of the forecast, we realized it wasn't going to be our day. The ground was already flooding, and the rain was extremely heavy. We sat in the car and meditated, and I have to tell you, it felt to me as if the place was full of earth energy. The problem is was I expecting that? The mound or hill is actually nothing to look at. It would be hard pushed to describe it as a hill at all in fact. It was raining so hard that I could not get a photo but it's a rather flat and nondescript area altogether.

So, we drove away and back to Budapest. Exploration of the site would need to await another time when I will take my rods and do some walking around looking for ley lines or energy lines and vortexes.

As we drove back very carefully as the road was flooding in many locations, I thought vaguely about my work with Perun – the thunder God of the Slavic hierarchy and remarked how funny it was that since I had been working with Perun, it was often very stormy weather and now a storm had kept us from visiting this site. I thought no more on it until later that night.

Arriving home in Brno, I went for a walk around the Castle. I would check in on my tree – yes, I talk to a tree – the same tree every day. Plainly, there had been a storm in Brno as well as a few branches and so on littered the pathway. However, when I got to MY tree, amongst thousands of trees, I discovered it had been struck by lightning.

Could it be that Perun had marked my tree in the time honored way? With his lightning. This was the tree that I touched every day and spoke to silently. I had been doing that for months. This was my tree, and I could only see this as confirmation of some sort of connection with Perun. To me, it seemed as if he had confirmed that we had indeed met in my exercises.

Transition

After several weeks of imagining myself as Perun, I thought perhaps it was time to balance out and try Veles. I set out on a walk with the idea that this really was my last time with Perun. Aptly, thundershowers were again all around, and I was treated to some amazing views of Perun's magnificence. He was truly all around me and everywhere I could see.

I visited my tree and decided to sit on the bench nearby. The timing of this moment was just as the Sun was setting above the Castle and so the path I had just walked was flooded with light and it was tempting to believe that I was being given a glimpse of the force of light that is behind Perun. As I meditated on the god and being the god, the word that came into mind was '*vigilance*' and as it did so the wind from the nearby storms rustled the treetops making it seem as if Perun was talking with me through the rustling of the trees. Vigilantly overseeing Creation – not His Creation however, it seemed to me, but one he now had responsibility for and over. It made sense.

As I continued my unhurried tour of the Castle grounds, he seemed to be all around me, and the air was filled with some sort of magic. It was a treat – a special treat – I think. The Cathedral was ablaze in the sun, yet a rain shower was behind it forming a dark shadow and there was a huge colorful rainbow opposite it. For Slavs, rain is seen as the result of Perun winning his eternal battle with Veles – the horned God of the underworld - and the rainbow seemed to me to celebrate his victory. Even a half moon shone down on this scene so that I knew the Goddess was also watching on.

A little later on, I came upon a blackbird. The little creature did not move as I approached and only when I tried to reach out did it move slightly away. I knew it had meaning for me by its behavior as it eyed me out of one bright eye and then the other before hopping a few steps across the path. We watched each other for about 5 minutes before I said goodbye and the bird rose up and away into the sky. In fact, this started a new phase of animal interaction with blackbirds. I felt like Dr. Doolittle walking and talking to butterflies, doves and blackbirds.

Is it too much to see the blackbird as a symbol of the underworld that awaits me as I transition over to Veles and the polarity of Earth and Water? I thought it an interesting encounter full of meaning and magic.

The following day, I cleansed and banished as having moved with Fire and Air for several weeks now and before switching polarities, I felt I must find the middle ground again – the plane of reflection. I see the relationship between Perun and Veles much like I see the relationship between Geburah and Chesed – in order to know one, one must experience both and the balance between.

It is also interesting that once again, I walk the hexagram[5] but this time, in a Slavic tradition circumnavigating the fire and Air triangles before doing the same with the Earth and Water triangles that together form the hexagram.

---

[5] The Mystical Hexagram. The Seven Inner Stars of Power, G. Michael Vasey & Sue Vincent. Asteroth's Books, 2015

My journey with Perun was almost over. I felt anger and an exhaustion, which I did not much like. I felt I now needed seek to balance things out with Veles the Slavic God of the underworld that engages in perpetual battle with Perun always ensuring equilibrium and balance. My focus on the Fire and Air of Perun needed a little balancing with the Water and Earth of Veles. Isn't this, after all, the meaning of the doves?

A week previously, a friend of mine and I had taken a trip to Holy Hill in Mikulov. It's a trip southwards from Brno toward the Austrian border – which you can actually see from the vantage point of Holy Hill. I wanted to introduce him to the dragon.

As we climbed the rough pathway up the 350m high hill, slipping and sliding on the hard angular limestone, it began to rain with a little thunder (Perun was everywhere during this time) and for a moment, we considered turning back. Instead, we sheltered in one of the mini chapels on the hill (stations of the cross). It was soon over, and the weather turned into a lovely early June evening.

I soon found what I think is a circular structure with central stones and the amazing Earth energy – a vortex – but it didn't feel quite so strong this time for some reason. My friend couldn't feel anything, but he could make out the circle of stones he said. We tried to dowse the spot, but he got no response at all while I had a very strong crossing over the stones. So, we got a bottle of water, laid it on the floor and did a quick dowsing training session – still he got nothing!

After some sandwiches and a bit of a meditation, we went off to explore a bit more of the hill. I hadn't managed that last time and still didn't really manage to see the entire hill this time either. I guess I will just have to go back again. We went to the imitation of the Holy Sepulcher and walked around it and then higher on to the hill and into the forest. The whole place has an energy about it, and I can imagine that the Church was very keen to claim it for their own and displace the pagans who used it for healing, fertility rites and probably more besides. The hill was originally Tanzberg Hill after all (Tancovat – to dance in Czech!).

I was pretty sure that we had found another energy center higher up the hill with very strong energy and it too appeared to be in a circular depression with rocks exposed at its center. Here, my friend did feel something – he said he could feel it in his chest – something. That tuned him in just a little because as we left and visited the original circle, he also felt something there. The dragon was making itself felt – possibly because we were acknowledging it.

I will just have to go back and spend an entire weekend exploring that hill. I cannot find much in terms of its history beyond the same basic information about the way of the cross and so on so more research is required. As always though, I came back home refreshed, re-energized and with a whole bunch of amazing pictures – oh, and a friend who maybe has started to become attuned to it all.

The Battle of the Gods

Perun is one side of a duality. His opposite number is Veles, god of earth, water, underworld and cattle amongst other things. Their battle is perpetual. Veles creeps up from the underworld and steals Perun's wife, children or cattle and takes them back to the underworld. There are many myths and tales about the two and their battles. In some, Perun's wife marries her captor and bears children to both gods. In others Perun's son marries Veles' daughter but ends up killing him annually due to his infidelity thus starting the battle once again. It is a classic pair of opposites in which perhaps we should look for the dynamic balance. Veles is the god of normal people, Perun is the god of warriors, princes and kings. Both are part of a larger whole I suspect.

Interestingly, Veles is also a trickster and a shapeshifter. If he is to be Perun's opposite then he represents chaos, earth and water. Veles is often seen as a serpent or a dragon and so we see an image of a knight spearing a dragon – that is Perun battling

Veles – and yet we have seen this image elsewhere with George or Michael and the dragon. In the end, Veles is always defeated by Perun and that victory is celebrated with rain. Then the cycle begins again. It is easy to see an annual seasonal cycle played out in this battle – one of light and the Sun god versus that of the dark and the underworld. One of winter death and springtime rejuvenation. It is the eternal duality of life and death, light and dark, order and chaos. However, one cannot exist without the other and what is important is the balance. The battle is seen in the lightening of thunderstorms. This seasonal duality can also be seen as a clash between fire and air over earth and water as well – it is an elemental battle. It is also worth reflecting on the hexagram and its hidden meanings.

For the Slavs, creation is a large Oak tree. On the top of that tree is the Eagle form of Perun and down amongst its roots is the serpent or dragon form of Veles. As Veles encroaches up the tree, Perun fights him with fire in the form of lightning bolts. This is the Slavic Tree of Life and the eternal battle between the dualities.

To me, Veles represents Earth energies symbolized in the form of the dragon or serpent which, when uncontrolled are chaotic. Perun, the god of order, uses his lance to 'kill' Veles the serpent but what he is doing I would suggest is bringing order to the chaotic energy and bringing that energy into equilibrium as a source of benefit. Perun works with the Earth energies and resolves it from a raw and chaotic form into something focused, ordered and positive.

We see this symbolism in other cultures and with other deities. It seems to be something of a common theme. I wonder if our ancestors knew of these powers and focused them and worked with them using stones and ritual?

Dragons and Stones

Velehrad is a small village with a significant past and is the center of an important pilgrimage in the Czech Republic. It is thought of as the 9th Century capital of the Slavic state of Great Moravia and recent archeological work has turned up some evidence of that period. These days though, it is known for the Basilica there. The Basilica of the Assumption and of St. Cyril and Methodius.

800 years ago, it is said that 12 Cistercian monks founded a monastery in Velehrad. A national pilgrimage now takes place every July which draws thousands of pilgrims. Pope John Paul II visited the monastery in 1990, his first visit outside the country after the fall of Communism. On July 5th every year, the site is inundated with pilgrims to celebrate the evangelization of the Slavs by the two Greek missionaries (Sts. Cyril and Methodius) in the 9th century. It features some Romanesque remnants and is a very beautiful building.

I noticed immediately that at the back of the church around the alter and in the Romanesque part, there are tremendous Earth energies. While we were there, several people had arrived seeking healing and undoubtedly, it is these pulsating energies that they seek and utilize. My friend, who usually professes to feel nothing at all, also felt the energy. I took a few moments to meditate and redirect the healing energies to another friend in need of it and trust that it found its way.

The energy is palpable and strong. I am convinced that this was an ancient site, and I am also convinced for some reason that it was a spring. Indeed, a waterway filled with clean and clear water runs past the basilica today. It also struck me that while the conventional wisdom might say the Velehrad means Great Castle or something similar, it might also be a corruption of Veles Hrad and refer to the Earth energies located there?

I feel the energy behind my neck usually as a sort of pressure and a tingling. As I get closer to its source, it becomes more throat located and sometimes I can feel a vibration that makes me want to emulate it as a deep guttural sound. I have never done so for fear people around me will believe me to be a lunatic but one day I will. Perhaps there is something shamanic about it.

My friend is gradually becoming acclimatized to my views on the magic of the land himself. He has a healthy degree of cynicism but having visited a couple of other sites with me this year, he is beginning to wonder about such things. So it was I felt a bit of a cosmic joke that as we walked around the Basilica and towards the end of the church with the energies, I looked up and saw a dragon.

"Is that a dragon?" I asked incredulously.

We both stopped and peered up and indeed, there was not one but two dragon heads on the ends of drainage pipes at that end of the Church hanging right over the part of the church where I had felt the energy strongest. My friend already knew that dragons often symbolize the Earth energies and so the point was not lost on him either.

"*Do you really think the builders knew about the energy?*" he asked.

"*I don't know for sure,*" I replied, "*but I have seen this before – clues hidden in plain sight.*"

As we took the tour of the foundations of the Basilica complete with exhibitions of various types. There was one exhibit that dealt with some archeological excavations of the site. It was a poster board collage of photographs and text in Czech, but I had a speaking guide in English to help me. There, in the center of the collage, was a floor tile with dragon. The archeologists expressed puzzlement as to '*why a symbol of evil was found in the Basilica/Monastery.*' As I pointed this out to my friend, "*Perhaps they once knew and maybe they still do.*"

There was the evidence. Right in front of us in the form a dragon on a floor tile.

Interestingly enough, there were also numerous examples of spirals on and around the church. The face of the church held two large spirals decorating it, a fountain outside the front of the church had spirals carved in its base and deep in the bowels of the church we found spiral designs on the stonework. Plainly, these spiral symbols were both ancient and modern. To me they symbolized the Earth energies there as a spiraling vortex. Along with the dragons, the suggested that there is a recognition of these natural energies in the Church.

The incredible wasn't over for the day however as the powers that be had something else in store for us. We decided to visit the underground part of the Church where we examined various pieces of masonry and so on before walking around the entire building in a maze of narrow and dark corridors and crypts. Again, I felt the energy strongest at the Romanesque part of the Church. There were some interesting symbols on old tombstones as well.

As we walked, I was talking to my friend about the butterflies. Indeed, I had been pointing out the butterflies all morning outside and marveling that there were so many at this time of the year. I had just told him about my last blog on Butterflies in fact when out of nowhere, a large black Butterfly or Moth suddenly appeared flying around INSIDE this part of the Church! It seemed like a final bit of proof, if any where needed. Another synchronicity to guide us on our way, and later that afternoon, we would need guiding as we searched for an ancient stone that didn't seem as if it wanted to be found.

Later, as we sat drinking soft drinks in the heat of the day and watching the innumerable butterflies flitting by we googled for other things to see in the Velehrad area. It was I who found reference to a dolmen – the King's Table (Kraluv Stul) in the area. I had never seen a stone in the Czech Republic – not one - so this seemed like a reasonable objective.

Quickly, we started looking for references to it and we both found it on Google maps and on several websites. Finishing our drinks, we got in the car and punched in the name of the village nearby where the stone was supposed to be. After several kilometers, I pulled over. Were we going to the right place? Still 33km and yet the stone was supposed to be nearby? We then discovered that there were two 'Jankovices' in the area and we had chosen the wrong one.

"These stones can be hard to find," I told my friend.

Arriving in Jankovice, we asked a man and his kids where the stone might be. He scratched his head and told us it was way back where we had started. This didn't appear to gel with our Google map GPS, so we decided to go with technology and go to the point indicated on Google maps. After driving along gravel and bumpy single track roads, we pulled up and headed into the forest convinced the stone was just a couple of hundred meters away.

"I told you these stones were hard to find," I said again.

"In fact, Sue often tells me they sometimes don't want to be found at all!" as we reached the spot on Google maps and yet saw nothing but forest.

No sign of any stone nor anything that looked like the pictures we had seen on internet sites. By this time, it was almost 5pm and with an hour trip home to Brno, I figured the stone was hiding from us and didn't want to be found.

A tad despondent, we got back in the car and drove along the road hoping perhaps to catch a glimpse of the stone in the vicinity but no such luck. We ended up in a small village well off the beaten track where we asked an older lady walking her dog. She had heard of it but didn't know where it was – we should try the pub she told us. At the pub, detailed directions were duly provided and off we went.

"Told you these stones don't like to be found," I said again.

After following the directions back to Jankovice, we came to a road up and over the hill that I didn't fancy driving on. It looked like one large pothole! However, one last try!

"It's hiding from us," I said.
The road was horrendous. I feared for my suspension and drove slowly until we reached its end.

"Perhaps I should have asked how far along this road it was," my friend said.

I nodded. Plainly, we had missed it and the stone was determined not to be found after all.

Despite this, we stopped at the T-junction at the end of that road and walked a couple of hundred meters into the forest either side in the vain hope of sighting it. We didn't but we did meet a family mushrooming who informed us that actually, it was just 250m away down the road.

We thanked them and jumped back in the car. The stone that didn't want to be found had been found!

According to one website[6], the King's table is shrouded in many legends, especially related to the Great Moravian past of Central Moravia. It is considered by some researchers to be a megalithic dolmen, which was supposed to be used to determine

---

[6] https://www.vychodni-morava.cz/cil/798

the days of the equinox and solstice. For this purpose, not only the marks on the stone block were to be used, but all the surrounding stones, formerly called "benches" as well though much of these were destroyed in 1870 during the construction of the road. Apparently it could have been a cult place, as some archaeological finds suggest. Undoubtedly, however, for centuries it served as a natural landmark and part of the boundary of the cadaster of the Velehrad monastery. It is first mentioned in the property deed of the monastery in 1228. As a natural landmark of the border, it remained at least until the 18th century, when a treaty on the mutual border between the Velehrad monastery and John of Rotal was concluded on October 6, 1706.

The king's table was the subject of much research. The first detailed description with a plan and a map was prepared and published by J. Chodníček in 1903. He was intensely interested in it and along with members of the Starý Velehrad association, conducted a survey there in 1929 publishing the results.

Antonín Zelnitius also published the results of his research in a separate paper in the mid-1940s. Exploratory archaeological probes were carried out in 1976 and 1977. At present, it is again in the center of attention of researchers and archaeologists who are trying to answer the question of the true origin and purpose of this monument. Previous surveys have confirmed the prehistoric landscaping and artificial location of the stone and one Dr. St. Štěrb managed to prove the carved characters inscribed on the main stone as Celtic runes.

The stone is a large block that immediately reminded me of a dragon's head or snake – some kind of serpent – though the sign there says that archeologists think it was a bull's head. It is within a circle of smaller stones but not in the center – it is offset to one side. My dowsing rods suggested to me the stone was displaced and should have been more or less in the center of the circle. It is marked with runes and as I touched it, it seemed to rock and sway under my touch. In the fading light late in the day, it seemed at times to be ablaze with solar energy. Earth and Solar energies melded together in a dragon's head circle.

I like to talk to stones and so I had a mental conversation with it. I talked about my desires, hopes and wishes as well as thought on someone else who needed the stone's attention. My friend also held a silent conversation with the rock. It listened in silence seeming to sway and rock under my touch. You could feel that there was a remnant of energy and that it appreciated our presence, but I also knew that it was damaged. The building of the road had disrupted its circumference and some stone had been removed for road foundation.

As we said goodbye and drove away in the fading light, I made a promise to return when I would have more time to sit, meditate and try to work with it further.

Recently, I revisited the King's Table. I needed to get into nature – into the bosom of the Goddess so to speak. For me, the connection to the land and to the Goddess is something that fades if I let it as I feel I am dragged away kicking and screaming by the mundane every day. Then suddenly, I wake up again to her call and realize it's been too long.

A few months ago, I got a message out of the blue from a guy in the USA. Over the past few months I hear from him periodically on Facebook Messenger. I don't know how he found me. He doesn't want anything except to tell me a few things it seems on a spiritual level – to share a few of his moments with the Goddess and connect. Last Sunday, out of the blue, he sent me a message…

"Hey, shaman! You need to get into nature."

He was right. So off I went. I took a friend along as well and we had a really nice day. We stopped off initially at Velehrad and explored the Earth energies either side of the alter. He could feel it too – he even picked it up at the same point I did, which was reassuring.

However, a couple of new thoughts about the place emerged as well. First, Velehrad could be thought of as 'Big Castle' or similar except there is no Castle and it isn't a big place. Though it could also be a pointer to its possible history as the capital of the ancient Moravian Kingdom as 'Great Castle' or similar. Now, I suspect the church is built on an ancient pagan center – a spring. It struck me, that perhaps it is actually named or the Slavic deity – Veles? Veles' Castle. That resonates with me.

Second, an exploration of the area around showed a stream passing close by and, as my friend remarked, the water was extremely 'clean' looking. I suspect it is spring water and hasn't traveled far. I suspect the site was a pagan site of worship and marked by a spring. Can't prove it but....

From there we went to Kraluv Stul. The so called King's Table and I dowsed along with my friend who was amazed to find he could do it and that he picked up the same features as I. Firstly, the vortex off center in the circle and not by the big stone at all and secondly, what seemed to be three energy lines passing through the vortex and.... marked by small stones in five of the six instances.

I again did a little meditation aided with a candle, some small polished stones and some water from a well in Yorkshire. I aimed healing energies where they were needed and made a few silent requests of my own. I had hoped the activity would change the energy of the place – wake it up so to speak – but I can't say I felt any difference. Who knows? Certainly, several other people visited that day and one or two of them demonstrated a reverence that suggested to me, the site was actively used already.

After a 10km hike through the misty, damp forest – through the bosom of the Goddess – we returned to the car for the trip home in the twilight. I felt a sense of renewal and connection again. And I made a vow, to try to stay more focused from now on.

Walking the Underworld

Meanwhile, my magical exercise continued, and I started to focus on Veles, God of the underworld and immediately, things flooded in. I mean engulfed me! Even something I haven't seen anywhere – that *v les* in Czech means *in the forest* and given the Pan-like nature of Veles... why wouldn't it? Veles – Ve les – in the forest. The green man, trickster. Water and earth – caves, underground, darkness... coming up and stealing children, women, crops and cattle – for what purpose? Netzach-like feelings.... Greenery. Horned cattle.

Veles is often seen in the form of a bear but as a shapeshifter, he could always be another animal too if he so chose. He was the trickster and mischevious. He is a horned god and most similar to Pan. He is also the god of the forest, nature, animals, agriculture, wisdom and magic. He is the patron of poets and musicians and Lord of Winter, the dead and crossroads. He is also the god of the underworld, caves, swamps and underground water. The Slavs view of the underworld was as a forest not as a dark place nor as a hell, and it coexisted with the world.

Veles is also found in other characters in Slavic mythology. He is Leshy or Lesnik (Les – forest in Czech), a protector of the forest who hides in tree trunks and under rocks while being hunted by Perun, the thunder god. It is another version of the battle between the dualities. In some instances, the same stories have Leshy portrayed as a dragon, or a snake.

For some, Veles is similar to Mercury, Odin or Hermes. His day is often cited as Wednesday, but other sources argue that Monday is Veles' day particularly in Russia where it is his day off and it is bad luck to die on a Monday as Veles isn't there to guide the soul.

He is portrayed often as a bald man, sometimes with horns. He is associated with horses, cows, goats, sheep, wolves, reptiles and yes, black birds including ravens and crows. He is the wise old man with horns and a staff and also the serpent at the base of the Tree. The trickster is associated with the liminal where Veles crosses the boundary between life and death, yet he lives among the dead in the underworld or inside the Earth. He is a god of boundaries. His feast day is February 11th.

Taking on Veles' form I found a bit more difficult and yet, once I was able to do it, it was rewarding. While I was imagining being Veles, black birds of various sorts suddenly where everywhere. One morning, as I lay in a hotel room asleep, I was awakened by a rapping at the window. As I fought to leave the dream – the very complex dream I had been dreaming – to see what the person knocking on the window wanted, it started to become obvious to me that, being located on the second floor of this hotel, I couldn't think of anyone who might be on our balcony at all at 6am! My slow awakening turned rather more to a sudden jump and all in one twist to look and see who it was rapping away loudly at our balcony window.

To my utter surprise, there was a very large black bird eyeing me from one of its blinking eyes while tapping its beak loudly against the window. The feeling of relief I felt on seeing it was a bird as opposed to something else was soon replaced by a sense of wonderment. Black birds and butterflies!

I was beset by butterflies and blackbirds. The butterflies were every color of the rainbow and ranged from tiny to quite large butterflies. I had remarked so often about the butterflies following me around that my vacation partner, now said it for me each time it occurred.

The blackbirds were a little rarer, but they came up to talk with me. There was the one that evening in Nin, Croatia that sat not three feet from me eyeing me up and 'talking' to me incessantly despite the crowd of passersby. This was the typical black bird encounter.

As I said above, the butterfly represents spiritual rebirth, transformation, creativity, endless potential, vibrant joy, change, ascension, and an ability to experience the wonder of life. I had also mused on whether the blackbird was a symbol of the underworld that awaits me as I transition over to the god form of Veles and the polarity of Earth and Water? What has been apparent is that this magic followed me to Croatia and my vacation!

On returning though back to Brno and resuming my walks around Špilbirk Castle, I realized that I had very much lost my connectedness to Veles, the Slavic God of the underworld, after a vacation punctuated summer. Hardly surprising I supposed as vacations were designed to be a switch off – a reset – if you will. I also wondered if I had ever really connected with Veles at all. With Perun, God of thunder and the sky, I felt His presence and His power very plainly. Veles was, as I said above, a bit trickier.

Tricky is an apt word as Veles is the trickster God in the Slavic pantheon. A horned God of the underworld but also of cattle and so on. As I walked, I decided to re visualize Him and as I did so, step into Him and walk as One.

It is strange but this simple imaginative act of magic sometimes brings the most profound results. I suddenly felt myself shorter and more squat. Muscular with a strange walking gait and two horns. The blackbird sat on my shoulder. A thought sprang into my mind almost immediately.

Veles, the trickster, can also represent our unconscious mind whereas Perun can represent the conscious mind. The unconscious mind where the shadow, the child and all of those other Jungian archetypes live. Suddenly, there was clarity which has now faded, and I now have difficulty explaining myself – or Veles. That happens.

In essence, I suddenly saw Veles' underworld as the unconscious mind. The unconscious mind is the great trickster is it not? It is where we hide as the shadow, the inner child and so on as I said above. Occasionally, our shadow will rise and peek through into the conscious mind who is the controlling side and pushes it right back again where it came from – the eternal battle between Perun and Veles can be thought of in this analogy.

So, as I take on the form of Veles, I slip into the underworld of my unconscious mind. Here there is trickery afoot but also there is great wisdom. The darkness holds secrets and getting to the bottom of those secrets is perhaps one aspect of the mastery of self.

The horns? Mostly I have seen horns as a representation of personal experience – the kind that entraps us and holds us back. The unconsciously learned behaviors and habits that bind us. Perhaps Veles' horns show this aspect of ourselves?

Interestingly, this is a theme explored in our book about the Hexagram.

It is also strange how themes repeat in various mythologies and pantheons as my mind conjured up Hathor – the horned Goddess – associated with cattle and welcoming the dead!

Suddenly I saw Veles as an invitation to explore the underworld – visit the interior of myself. The unconscious mind can be our enemy – fear, unresolved emotions, our inner demons reside in its darkness. It can also be our liberator, symbolically showing us who we are and informing us what we should be.

In a simple moment of imagination, I realized I had connected with Veles.

I've written many times about seeing Butterflies and even having them land on me. Well, here we were in mid-September and everywhere I went was filled with Butterflies of some shape or description. They fluttered across my path as I walk my daughter's dog or along the side of the road as I drive my car. They are everywhere and I cannot ever recall seeing so many for so much of the year.

The black birds also reminded me of the crows that live on the Castle hill above me. In the winter and while the shaman was doing his thing, the crows where everywhere and by summer, they had long gone. As I write in late November, they are back to remind us that this is the time of Veles.

The Gates to the Underworld

Most people love a creepy story especially if it comes wrapped in mystery and features castles, strange creatures and strange stories. Houska Castle in the Czech Republic has been quite the creepy story making appearances on all sorts of paranormal podcasts and even an entire episode of Ghost Hunters International.

It is a story that I too utilized in my Czech ghost stories book wrapped in sensationalism, mystery and horror.

Houska Castle is known as the Gateway to Hell. A reputation it has built up over the years around a story that appears to have been repeated and embellished with each telling and retelling. It now provides the owners of the castle some income as streams of tourists visit the castle and, its rather tacky exhibits. As I myself wrote in *The Czech Republic – The Most Haunted Country in the World*.

Over 1000-years ago, much of the Czech countryside would have been dense forest. In the Houska area, those forests would have been dark, gloomy, damp, and eerie as the area is famous for its sandstone formations known as 'Skaly'. The sandstone in the area erodes out into block-like formations that jut out ominously in many locations, creating an eerie but beautiful landscape. Millennia ago, this landscape would have been like an alien world for the sparse populace in which the imagination would and could run riot! There were few settlements and fewer people who still clung to many pagan beliefs about woodland spirits, demons and ghosts. Not surprisingly, the area developed an evil reputation. Demons and half-human monsters were said to roam the deeply incised, tree-covered valleys, seeking human and animal victims and warm blood.

The discovery of a deep crack or fissure in the sandstone certainly wouldn't have helped matters much in terms of the areas' terrifying reputation. Efforts to fill the fissure with stones and boulders failed. In fact, they had no impact whatsoever. The fissure seemed endless; a crack of doom in the Earth's surface from which that knows what monsters, elementals, and spirits emerged? Rumors suggested that this fissure without end was a gateway to hell and that demons and spirits used it as a route to Satan's fiery regime for wicked hell-bound human souls and the innocent victims of demonic activity in the area. Local farms mysteriously lost animals and passersby avoided it in the darkness.

Something had to be done and at some point in the 900's it seems as if a Chapel was built over the crack in the Earth in an attempt to close it and lock out the demons. In fact, no one is really sure when the Castles' structure really was built, as mysteriously, the records have all disappeared. This fact is even more dramatic given that the Czech Republic is littered with fairytale-like Castles each with a thoroughly documented and proud history. The first mentioned structure on the site however was a small wooden fort in the 9th Century though it is believed that a structure might have existed on the site since the 6th Century. Part of Houska's mystery is that it is the exception to the rule in not having a documented history. In fact, it doesn't even appear on some maps as if it were meant to be a secret that was kept secret. The story of Houska becomes even stranger however, for as the structure was being built, the Landlord agreed that whichever condemned man would be lowered on a rope into the crack in the rock to describe what he saw there, would be freed. A volunteer was lowered only a few feet into the hole in the Earth before he started screaming hysterically. He was immediately retrieved and found to have suddenly developed snow-white hair, aged at least 30-years and had become quite mad. He died the following day without divulging what horrors he had seen in the gate to hell. One can imagine that work resumed on the Castle with even more urgency than before.

The Castle or structure that was built there was also very strange. It had defensive structures facing inside the castle as opposed to outside, to keep out intruders. Rather, it seemed designed to keep something in. Although it had several floors, there were no stairs connecting the floors and additionally, it had fake windows in the upper stories. It was a very strange Castle indeed. Added to that was its' location, which was far from anywhere and not on any pathway or road. It did not have a source of water and it was for all intents and purposes a castle that was built where no castle would normally ever be constructed.

The fissure or endless hole apparently now lies beneath the floors of a small chapel. Painted on the walls of the inside of the chapel are rather strange designs that include the only known example of a female left-handed centaur shooting a man with an arrow. On another wall, is the image of St. Michael plunging his lance into the mouth of a fearsome dragon. Other images include St. Christopher, an angel weighing human souls and the Christ. Having stood in the Chapel myself, I can tell you that there *is an energy there that after only a short while becomes unbearable. I had a headache for several hours after leaving. Interestingly, these murals add mystery to the Castle as being left-handed in medieval times was thought to be a sign of evil (the left-hand path) and St. Michael was the Archangel tasked with fighting hell's hoards. Despite all of this, strange sounds, moans and screams are said to be heard coming from below the Chapel and people have claimed to see demonic entities there, including a strange creature that looks like a cross between a human, frog and giant bulldog.*

I revisited Houska to show my son visiting from the USA recently and it suddenly found a place in this account for reasons that hopefully will become obvious. I had also visited it in 2019 when unfortunately it was closed. In both instances, I could feel the energy probably 10km away. It is a powerful and somewhat ominous energy that I feel in my throat and neck. Unfortunately, the castle was closed again but we got a good look at the place – false windows behind which there are thick walls, one side built on a precipice while the other is approachable up a gentle hill. We could at least walk around the outside in the fading light of the day and I had brought my dowsing rods!

The dowsing rods showed us two meter plus thick energy lines at least enter the castle – or did. The entry of one line was defended by a large stone cross that I hadn't noticed before while the other appeared marked by an ornate and large stone placed on the ground aligned with the line.

The second energy line marked by a strange stone. But these days, I think I have learned to read things a bit differently. If you take away all of the sensationalism around the place, what do we have left? A fissure in the rock, a chapel in a castle with strange images, energy lines apparently blocked off? very strong earth energies.

The chapel has an image of St, Michael spearing the dragon and as we have seen, the dragon is a symbol of earth energies and the spearing of a dragon is that of bringing earth energies under control. The left handed female centaur drawing reinforces the point as a centaur also embodies strong earth energies. Even the St. Christopher adorning the wall can be seen as offering the perspective of something changed from bad to good as St. Christopher is often seen as a dog-headed giant who was redeemed and given human form after he carried the Christ-child across a river.

My current theory of Houska isn't as sensational as the mass of stories on the internet. I think that this is a place of tremendous earth energies emanating from the sandstone there. Those energies can be felt for kilometers around the place and gave it a strange and mysterious, powerful vibe. I think that the attempt to block the energy with the chapel/castle and the stones blocking the energy lines has disrupted the natural flow of these energies and this is usually enough to give the energy a negative feel. Disrupted energies also attract entities possible explaining the ghost and creature sightings there. Indeed, a local we met walking her dog told us matter of factly, there were many strange ghost sightings in the vicinity.

The earliest written reference to the castle says that it keeps *"something that must not be named"* from escaping into the outside world. I am unable to find any pre-Christian information, but I wonder if the earth energy was that something unnamed? Was it or had it been a pagan Slavic site utilized for that energy? I will continue to research it to see if I can find out. Meanwhile, no wonder the place was used by the Nazis and other occultists – the energy there would lend itself to such work especially as that energy has been throttled and subverted.

It somehow also seemed apt to me that here, the famed gate to hell located in Czechia, was a site of strong Earth energies that pervaded the surroundings perhaps with a chaotic and liminal energy and environment. Now doesn't that remind us of Veles, the god of that underworld? I guess you wouldn't be surprised to learn that while we visited Houska, a huge storm blew up" Nope? Me neither.

Next Steps

My experiences with Perun and Veles bore fruit and their forces became a part of my everyday life both spiritually and physically with butterflies, black birds, doves and so on. I again felt the connections with this land and saw glimpses of an understanding of a culture alien to myself and yet not so far from my own Celtic and Nordic roots. I feel that the grand experiment paid off handsomely. Plainly, I cannot pass on everything in this book. Not because I don't want to or should not. More because words are not enough.

I have now devised my next adventure. I wish to explore the goddess and her three aspects. I have renewed my love of nature and the goddess and I feel closer to her than ever before. She occupies my dreams. She is inside my mind and my heart. So, as 2021 begins, I will take on the three Slavic aspects of the Goddess in turn, in their season and see what happens.

Now this isn't going to be easy as there are a lot of goddesses in the Slav hierarchy and it isn't necessarily clear which is which. Also, there is an aspect to the Slavic goddesses in the form of water spirits called Rusalki who can be pretty lethal to us men. So, I need to watch out and be careful.

I shall work with Vesna, Živa and Morena where Vesna is the maiden and the goddess of Spring, Živa, the lady of the summertime and the harvest – the living one, followed by Morena, Goddess of death and winter. I have begun my preparation and I will align the work with the Moons and also the solstices and equinoxes.

Meanwhile, if you want to follow my progress on this year long journey, please visit my blog at garymvasey.net where I will most likely post about it.

About G. Michael Vasey

With over 40 books in print, Gary is an established author with notable contributions in the areas of the paranormal, metaphysics, poetry, and business. He is also a collector of strange stories at My Haunted Life Too[7]. In 2016, he resumed his interest in music and has released two albums of self-penned and self-performed songs that are available at all digital music stores. Since then, he has been churning out catchy songs at a rapid rate and captured the interest of a growing audience.

He was born in the city of Hull in England, and grew up in East Yorkshire, the eldest of three boys. Growing up can be extremely tough for any kid, but imagine growing up around poltergeist activity and ghosts? G. Michael Vasey had exactly that kind of childhood, experiencing ghosts, poltergeists, and other strange and scary, supernatural phenomena. In fact, he seemed to attract it, developing an interest in

---

[7] www.myhauntedlifetoo.com

the occult and supernatural at an early age and he has been fascinated ever since.

His "My Haunted Life" trilogy has been highly successful–reaching number one on bestseller lists on both sides of the Atlantic. Now he is also presenting the stories of others. His book about the Black Eyed Kids is currently available on Amazon and continues to capture the morbid interest of hundreds of fans. It's a must-read for anyone with an interest in the strange happenings of the paranormal world.

Then there's "*The Pink Bus and Other Strange Stories from LaLa Land*," a book that lifts the veil on one of the biggest mysteries in human history–the process of death, and what happens to our souls when we die. His novella – The Last Observer – won critical praise and is a twisty story about the nature of reality and magic. His most recent books have included a tour of the supernatural side of the Czech Republic, a set of Kindle shorts on topics like

Poltergeists, Ghosts of the Living (bilocation) and The BEK now issued as a compilation volume, a new book of poetry, a look at the recently headlining topic of paranormal sex and, the Halloween Vault of Horror, a new collection of true paranormal stories.

He has appeared on numerous radio shows such as

* Mysterious Radio,
* Jim Harold's paranormal podcasts,
* The Knight's Pub,
* True Ghost Stories Online and
* X Radio with Rob McConnell

Whether you've heard one of G. Michael Vasey's radio appearances, or read one of his books over the shoulders of an avid reader on the bus, or whether you've simply got an interest in the paranormal and stumbled upon this page... You are going to pulled into the paranormal world of G. Michael Vasey, and you will be hooked.

You can discover much more about the supernatural at www.gmichaelvasey.com or read true scary stories at www.myhauntedlifetoo.com.

Gary has also studied magic for many years with organizations like AMORC, CR&C, SOL and The Silent Eye. He is a second degree initiate of SOL and performed as a supervisor for the school for many years. He has written several books on magic including The Mystical Hexagram penned with Sue Vincent and The New You.

Other Books

- **Chasing the Shaman** (ebook, paperback)
- **The Scary Best of My Haunted Life Too** (ebook, paperback)
- **Motel Hell** (ebook)
- **G. Michael Vasey's Halloween Vault of Horror** (ebook)
- **The Seduction of the Innocents** (ebook,

audiobook and Paperback)

- **The Chilling, True Terror of the Black-Eyed Kids – A Compilation** (Paperback, Audiobook and ebook)
- **Poltergeist – The Noisy Ghosts** (ebook)
- **Ghosts of the Living** (ebook)
- **Your Haunted Lives 3 – The Black Eyed Kids** (ebook)
- **Lord of the Elements (The Last Observer 2)** (ebook and Paperback)
- **True Tales of Haunted Places** (ebook)
- **The Most Haunted Country in the World – The Czech Republic** (ebook, paperback, audiobook)
- **Your Haunted Lives – Revisited** (ebook and Audiobook)
- **The Pink Bus** (ebook and audio book)
- **Ghosts in The Machines** *(ebook and audiobook)*
- **The New You** *(Paperback, ebook and audiobook)*
- **God's Pretenders – Incredible Tales of**

Magic and Alchemy *(ebook and audiobook)*

- **My Haunted Life – Extreme Edition** *(Paperback, audiobook and ebook)*
- **My Haunted Life 3** *(Audiobook and eBook)*
- **My Haunted Life Too** *(Audio book and ebook)*
- **My Haunted Life** *(ebook and audiobook)*
- **The Last Observer** *(Paperback, ebook and Audiobook)*
- **The Mystical Hexagram** *(Paperback and ebook)*
- **Inner Journeys – Explorations of the Soul** *(Paperback and ebook)*

Other Poetry Collections

- **Slavic Tales** (ebook and paperback)
- **Reflections on Life: Spiritual Poetry** (ebook and paperback)
- **The Dilemma of Fatherhood** (ebook)
- **Death on The Beach** *(ebook)*

- **The Art of Science** *(Paperback and ebook)*
- **Best Laid Plans and Other Strange Tails** *(Paperback and ebook)*
- **Moon Whispers** *(Paperback and ebook)*
- **Astral Messages** *(Paperback and ebook)*
- **Poems for the Little Room** *(Paperback and ebook)*
- **Weird Tales** *(Paperback and ebook)*

All of G. Michael's Vasey's books can be obtained from many retailers and book selling sites. He offers signed and dedicated paperbacks from his website at https://www.garymvasey.com